PIVOT POINT

PIVOT POINT FUNDAMENTALS: COSMETOLOGY
LIFE SKILLS

1st Edition
4th Printing, October 2021
Printed in China

Pivot Point International, Inc.
Global Headquarters
8725 West Higgins Road, Suite 700
Chicago, IL 60631 USA

847-866-0500
pivot-point.com

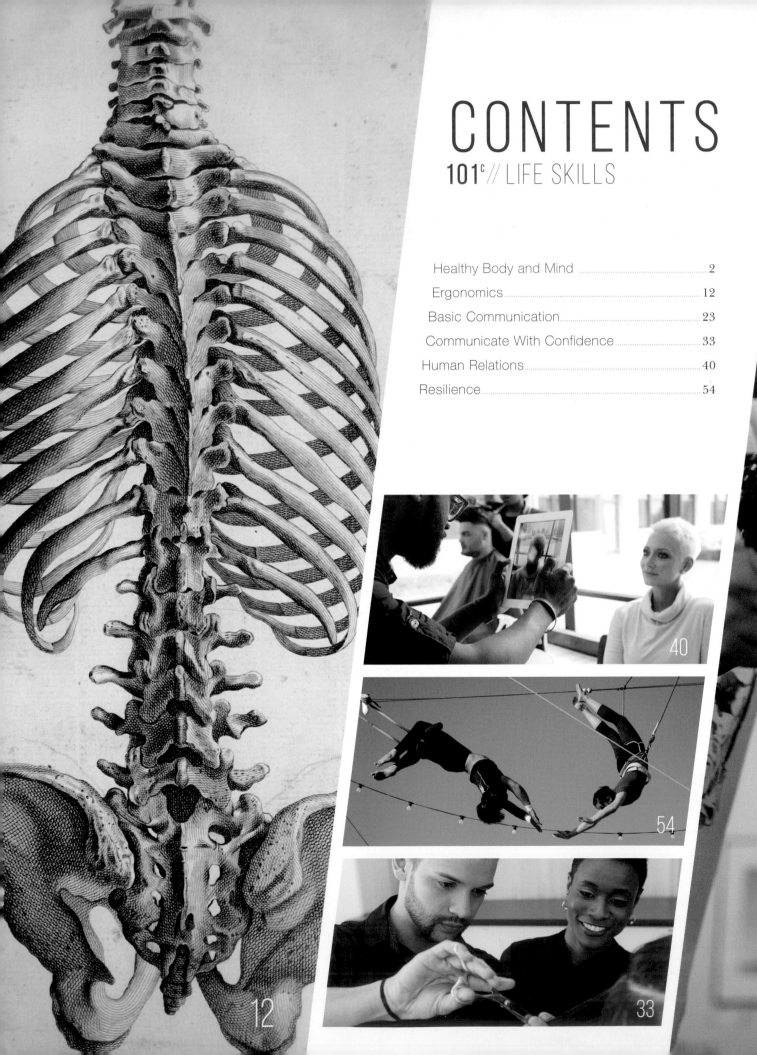

CONTENTS
101ᶜ // LIFE SKILLS

40

54

33

12

23

2

101ᶜ.1
HEALTHY BODY & MIND//

EXPLORE //

Has someone in your past helped you improve your body or mind?

INSPIRE //

A lifelong commitment is necessary for salon professionals who want to maintain a healthy body and mind. Long hours of physical work with the hands, sitting, standing and a demanding public call for an established wellness routine.

ACHIEVE //

Following this lesson on *Healthy Body and Mind*, you'll be able to:

>> State the recommended number of hours to sleep per night

>> Identify the effects of regular exercise

>> Describe the value of a balanced diet

>> Explain the differences between personal and public hygiene

>> Summarize the elements involved in presenting a professional image

FOCUS //

HEALTHY BODY AND MIND

Rest and Relaxation

Exercise

Nutrition

Hygiene

Image

101°.1 HEALTHY BODY & MIND

■ Establishing routines to maintain a healthy body and
■ mind is the first step toward professional development.

Dedication to each of these areas will help ensure that you are on the right track.
What routines do you currently use to help you achieve a healthy body and mind?

Cosmetology is the art and science of beauty care. Cosmetology professionals, also called salon professionals, are people who openly express the value of their chosen field in the way they:

>> Work, communicate and conduct themselves

>> Believe in the value of bringing beauty to the lives of others

>> Achieve the highest standards of beauty care and professional behavior

>> Attain a healthy body and mind

REST AND RELAXATION

Sufficient rest and relaxation are as necessary as work for a healthy, happy life.

>> Sleep helps relieve the frustrations and tensions that are a result of everyday activities.

>> **Most people need 6-8 hours of sleep or they become fatigued and cannot function properly.**

>> **Rest and relaxation are necessary to prevent fatigue.**

EXERCISE

A regular exercise program will help you feel better, look better and work better. Your muscles, heart muscles included, need to be in their best possible condition.

Exercise is a proven method through which you can:

>> **Keep your muscles toned**

>> **Stimulate the blood circulation in your body**

>> **Encourage proper functioning of organs**

>> **Equip your body to better cope with stressful situations**

DISCOVER**MORE**

Round out your exercise program by remembering to exercise your mind also. Reading is the best form of exercise for the mind.

Get Away From it All

Once you begin your career, being able to "get away from it all" with activities such as reading a good book, listening to music, or watching TV will be very important for a healthy body and mind. It will also be important to take the time to set up an exercise program you will enjoy, such as a brisk daily walk, bicycling or hiking on the weekend, or yoga to keep your body toned and in shape. Just getting out a few times a week to enjoy the fresh air will allow you to return to work refreshed. Remember, you have chosen a profession that is very physical and the better conditioning you give your body, the greater the chances of your success and health.

NUTRITION

A balanced diet is essential for your personal and professional well-being, providing energy for the body to use and may help to prevent certain diseases.

A typical day in the salon can be demanding and your diet may be one of the most important factors for your success.

Almost all foods contain mixtures of the three energy nutrients:

>> Carbohydrates
>> Fats
>> Proteins

The energy they contain is measured in calories. The body uses this energy in several ways to:

>> Heat itself
>> Build its structures
>> Move its parts during exercise and activities

The energy may also be stored in body fat for later use. In addition to the energy nutrients, other essential nutrients include vitamins, minerals and water.

	CALORIES BURNED	
ACTIVITY (1 HOUR)	140 LB. PERSON	195 LB. PERSON
Aerobics, general	381	531
Basketball game	508	708
Bicycling, 10 mph, leisure	254	354
Cleaning house, general	222	310
Gardening, general	318	443
Horseback riding, walking	159	221
Jogging	445	620
Judo, karate, kick boxing, tae kwon do	636	885
Mowing lawn	350	487
Rope jumping, moderate	636	885
Running, 6 mph (10 minute mile)	636	885
Tennis, singles	508	708

Data is based on research from Medicine and Science in Sports and Exercise, the "Official Journal of the American College of Sports Medicine."

DISCOVER**MORE**

Dietary Reference Intakes (DRIs) are developed and published by the Institute of Medicine (IOM). DRIs indicate the nutrient needs of healthy populations. It makes good sense to follow these nutrient recommendations to promote good health.

HYGIENE

Hygiene is the science that deals with healthful living.

>> The practice of public hygiene is important because it helps to preserve the health of the community.

>> Impure air from poor ventilation, inadequate lighting, improper disinfection practices, and improper storage or use of food are the primary health hazards against which health officials expect you to protect clients.

>> Your job as a professional is to protect and serve the public.

SALON**CONNECTION**

Clients Depend on You

The fact that you are in training to be a licensed professional says that you are ready to recognize that your clients can depend on you to protect them from health and safety hazards they might experience in the salon.

CHECKLIST FOR PERSONAL HYGIENE PLAN:

- Regular Bathing
- Deodorant
- Mouthwash
- Perfume or Cologne
- Clean Clothing

Your individual system for maintaining your cleanliness and health is your **personal hygiene**.

In your work, you'll be close to your clients constantly. Keep in mind:

» Scents or soil that wouldn't ordinarily be noticed now can be.

» Establishing and maintaining a personal hygiene routine is essential if you expect your clients to enjoy your company and want to come back.

Though you might like to believe otherwise, all bodies produce odors. Guidelines for preventing unpleasant body odors include:

» Bathing regularly using soap

» Applying deodorant following bathing

» Avoiding excess use of perfume or cologne

» Washing clothing when soiled

Few people consider the cleanliness of the inside of their shoes. Yet unclean shoes and the length of time you wear them in a day can create foot odor if not checked. A little talc or foot deodorant can often help.

The food you eat and the state of your health affect the condition of your breath.

» Eating too much garlic could result in unpleasant body smells from perspiration, along with **bad breath, referred to as halitosis** (hal-eh-**TOH**-sis).

» A sore throat often produces unpleasant odors from your mouth.

» Brush your teeth as often as you can each day, certainly after every meal, and use mouthwash.

Consider all potential hygiene problems and establish a personal hygiene plan that addresses them daily. Your personal hygiene contributes to or detracts from your success.

IMAGE

The salon business is a service business; therefore, close attention to personal grooming is a priority. Care of your hair, skin, hands, feet and clothing needs to be of the utmost importance. Follow the basic guidelines listed in this section to help ensure your professional image.

Oral hygiene refers to maintaining healthy teeth and keeping the breath fresh.

>The most beautiful hair is clean and healthy hair.<

HAIR CARE

As a salon professional, of course, the condition of your hair is of particular importance.
A daily hair care program is essential for you.

Your own hair design communicates your professional expertise. Your hair design should be
fashionable, yet include any necessary modification that will allow it to better suit your face.

SKIN CARE AND MAKEUP

The proper care of your skin isn't limited to the products you put on it.

>> **Healthy, glowing skin is equally dependent on good nutrition, exercise and rest.**

>> As a salon professional, you will need to keep your skin looking its best.

>> Research the variety of skin care products now available and find the regimen best suited for your skin type.

>> It will become increasingly apparent to you how personal skin care knowledge will be an advantage when recommending skin care products for your future clients.

Cosmetics can enhance attractive facial features and help balance proportions that aren't quite right. Just as one can contour a face with creative hair color techniques, one can contour facial features with the careful use of cosmetics.

When fashion trends change, the popular makeup look usually changes, too. In your profession, it's as important to update your use of cosmetics as it is to wear a hair design that reflects the correct fashion look.

It's important that you learn to modify current cosmetic trends into looks that are flattering for you.

The basics of makeup application never change:

>> **Foundation should match your skin tone.**

>> **Contouring with light colors always broadens.**

>> **Contouring with dark colors always narrows.**

> Cosmetics can enhance attractive facial features and help balance proportions that aren't quite right.

CONTOUR TIPS

Area of Concern	Goal	Contour Tip
Overly Wide Jaw	Visually appear more narrow	Apply darker contour cream to the outer areas of the jawline.
Narrow Forehead	Visually broaden	Apply lighter cosmetic shades along the hairline.
Small Lips	Visually appear larger	Create a lipstick line just outside the natural lip line.
Large Lips	Visually appear more narrow	Create a lipstick line just inside the natural line of the lips.

Cosmetic shades change. So does the fashionable use of makeup—from obvious and dramatic to light and natural. Master the basic techniques and then you will be able to learn how to apply makeup to suit any fashion trend in the manner that will complement you best.

HANDS

Your hands will touch many people during the course of your career, so they need to be smooth, soft, immaculately clean, and well-manicured. Maintaining attractive hands is particularly challenging for a salon professional because the services you'll perform will often find your hands in water and/or require the use of chemicals.

Guidelines for hands include:

>> Wearing protective gloves when using chemicals

>> Using moisturizing lotions frequently

>> Keeping your nails attractively manicured

>> Avoiding wearing rings that can chafe or irritate

>> Taking the best care of your hands that you can

FEET

A great deal of your time as a salon professional will be spent standing on your feet.

>> You will need to take proper care of your feet.

>> Practice good posture and **wear good-fitting, low, broad-heeled shoes.**

>> Make sure your feet are dried thoroughly after bathing to prevent fungus infections like athlete's foot.

To keep your feet at their best, schedule regular pedicures that will include cleansing, removal of callused skin, massage and toenail trims. If you develop bunions, corns or ingrown toenails, etc., see a podiatrist (foot doctor).

CLOTHING

Your clothing should be freshly washed, or cleaned and pressed.

>> Unsightly rings around the collar or the armpit are not acceptable.

>> Shoulder fit should be loose enough to allow easy movement.

>> No article of clothing should be uncomfortably or unflatteringly tight.

>> Shoes look best when clean and polished.

Dress for Success

Your wardrobe should be selected to incorporate current trends into a statement consistent with your personal sense of style. You're in an age of fashion that shows a variety of designer looks for any given season.

>> Some looks will be more popular than others, but if the one that's popular doesn't look good on you, go on to something else.

>> Exercise good sense by taking into consideration your height and silhouette when selecting fashions.

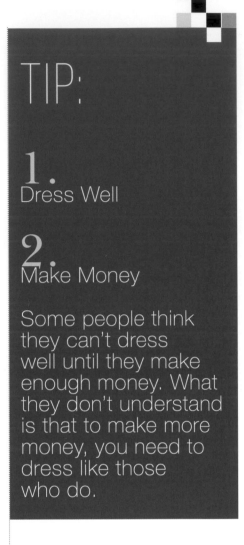

TIP:

1.
Dress Well

2.
Make Money

Some people think they can't dress well until they make enough money. What they don't understand is that to make more money, you need to dress like those who do.

SALON**CONNECTION**

Dress Code

Many schools and salons have a dress code for their employees or students. Follow it with careful consideration of your personal sense of style and fashion, and you'll look like the professional you aspire to be.

POSTURE

The need for good posture goes beyond just standing correctly. Good posture enhances your physical well-being. As a professional designer, you'll be on your feet every day. As you work with clients throughout the day you'll bend and stretch and stoop. As you restock inventory, *it may be necessary for you to lift boxes as heavy as 50 pounds*. **Maintaining good posture and moving properly will:**

» **Protect you from muscle strain and potential injury**

» **Reduce physical fatigue**

» **Present an attractive image**

LESSONS LEARNED

The recommended number of hours to sleep per night is 6-8 hours.

The effects of regular exercise include blood circulation stimulation, proper organ function, muscle tone and stress relief.

The value of a balanced diet includes personal and professional well-being, energy for the body, and the possibility of preventing certain diseases.

The difference between personal and public hygiene is that personal hygiene refers to maintaining one's own health and cleanliness, while public hygiene refers to preserving the health of the community.

The elements involved in presenting a professional image include hair care, skin care and makeup, hands, feet, clothing and posture.

DO'S AND DON'TS FOR GOOD POSTURE

DO

Do use the height adjustments provided on equipment so you can work on your client's hair without stooping over or reaching up.

Do keep your head up, your chin level, your shoulders relaxed but straight and your abdomen held flat when standing.

Do keep your feet and knees together, feet on the floor, when sitting, and sit well back in the chair.

DON'T

Don't slump over the work area. Instead, bend forward at the waist holding your shoulders straight.

Don't bend at the waist when lifting objects from the floor. Bend at the knees to lower your whole body.

Don't, when standing, place more of your weight on one leg than the other. Choose positions that distribute your weight evenly.

Your dedication to a healthy body and mind will improve your health and help you present a professional image.

101ᶜ.2
ERGO-
NOMICS

EXPLORE //

Ever wonder what methods and techniques professional athletes use to keep their bodies in top performance shape?

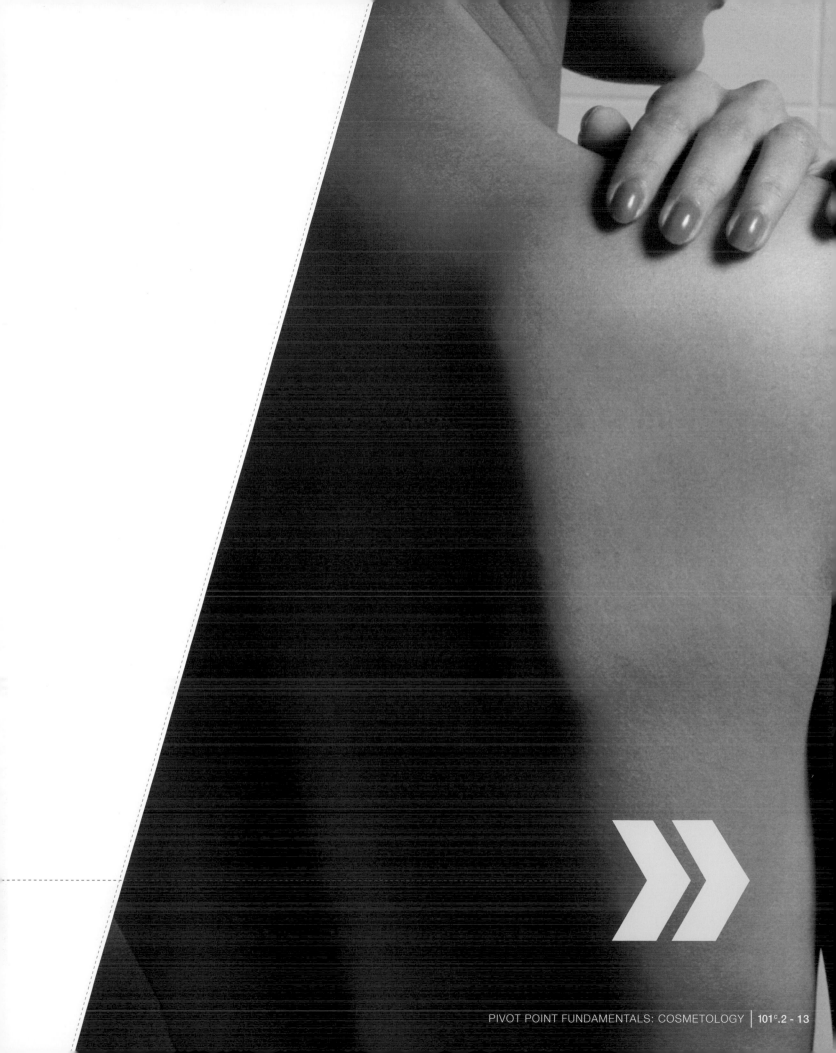

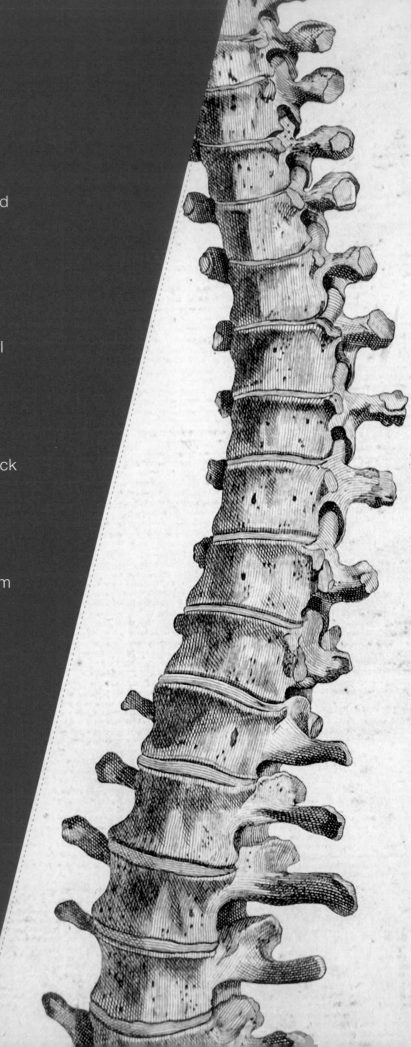

INSPIRE **//**

The steps you take today to sustain your body's condition will help ensure a long and prosperous career in the beauty industry.

ACHIEVE **//**

Following this lesson on *Ergonomics*, you'll be able to:

>> Explain the importance of ergonomics and how it affects a salon professional's job performance

>> Identify common causes of neck and back pain and ways to prevent it

>> State common causes of foot and leg problems and ways to prevent them

>> Compare common causes of hand and wrist problems and ways to prevent them

>> Cite common causes of shoulder strain and ways to prevent it

FOCUS **//**

ERGONOMICS

Neck and Back

Foot and Leg

Hands and Wrists

Shoulders

101^c.2 ERGONOMICS

Have you ever experienced muscle aches or pains after doing personal chores or activities? Maybe after a workout at the gym or washing the car? Once those tasks were done, your body had time to rest. In the salon you'll spend long hours standing, bending, reaching and performing repetitive motions. These activities can cause pain, fatigue and sometimes serious injury in various parts of the body that develop slowly over a long period of time. Better work habits, proper equipment and appropriate body movements can prevent this.

The science of **ergonomics** looks at how you work; the body movements, positions, tools and equipment you use; and the effect these things have on your health and comfort. New tools and equipment continually being developed to support health issues related to ergonomics can extend the longevity of your salon career.

NECK AND BACK

Your spine runs from the top of your neck down to your lower back. It is made up of many bones called vertebrae, one below another. Between each pair of vertebrae are joints and discs that give your neck and back flexibility, so they can move.

Discs are flexible because they have a jelly-like substance inside. Both joints and discs can be hurt if you strain or squeeze them. Prolonged bending or twisting of the body can cause pain in your neck, back, arms or legs, especially if a disc ruptures and the jelly inside leaks out.

Neck and back strain can occur if you:

>> Bend forward when performing a service

>> Twist your body to get closer to a client or to reach for something

>> Reach overhead for supplies

>> Arch (lean) backward because you've been standing for a long time

>> Stand for a long time in high-heeled shoes

RECOMMENDATIONS TO PREVENT NECK AND BACK PROBLEMS

General

>> Work with your back straight; stand with feet parallel to hips.

>> Keep your back straight and abdominal muscles pulled in while seated to prevent slouching; sit squarely in your chair.

>> Hold your back erect, bend at the knees and use the thigh muscles when lifting heavy objects or picking up articles from the floor, rather than bending at the waist.

>> Bend your knees slightly and pull in your abdominal muscles when you have to reach up. Called a pelvic tilt, this motion keeps you from arching backward.

>> Stand on a footstool when reaching for supplies on a high shelf.

>> Sit with legs uncrossed and feet flat on the floor; avoid sitting in a chair sideways; move the entire body when turning, rather than turning at the waist.

Service-Specific

>> Use a free-standing sink (also known as a backwash system) for shampooing.

>> Adjust the height of the client's chair.

>> Tilt the client's head to a position that is comfortable for you.

>> Have clients with very long hair stand up while you work.

>> Use a chair with a tilted seat when doing manicures or sit on a wedge-shaped cushion that tilts your body forward.

>> Place one foot on a stool or on a rung under the client's chair when you stand for long periods of time.

>> Position facial chair or bed and facial machines close to you to avoid unnecessary reaching.

>> Perform stretching exercises on short breaks and alternate services when possible to avoid repetitive motions.

Adapted from Health and Safety for Hair Care and Beauty Professionals, Labor Occupational Health Program, University of California at Berkeley.

**Neck
Stretches**

A few simple neck stretches done periodically
during the day can help alleviate neck pain. When applicable,
hold each position for 15 seconds and make sure your shoulders stay still.

1. Bring your chin to your chest.
2. Turn your head to the left, then the right.
3. Bring your left ear toward your left shoulder. Repeat on the right side.
4. Rotate your head clockwise five times while standing.
   Repeat in the opposite direction. //

Adapted from Free4m: The Holistic Approach to Hairdressing.

FOOT AND LEG

Standing for a long time may cause your feet and ankles to swell, and put you at risk for getting varicose veins (swollen veins). Also, if any part of your foot is under pressure, you can get calluses or skin irritation at the pressure point.

Foot and leg problems can occur if you:

>> Stand for long periods, especially on a hard floor

>> Wear high-heeled shoes, especially if the toes are pointed

>> Wear shoes with poor arch support or hard soles

>> Wear shoes that don't fit well

RECOMMENDATIONS TO PREVENT FOOT AND LEG PROBLEMS

General

>> Don't stand or sit for long periods of time. Change positions frequently.

>> Wear comfortable, rubber-soled shoes or low, broad-heeled shoes with good arch support. Avoid high heels and shoes with pointed toes.

>> Use shock-absorbing inserts inside your shoes.

>> Use an anti-fatigue or comfort mat instead of standing on a hard floor.

>> Use support hose to reduce leg swelling.

Service-Specific

>> Hydraulic chairs for clients should adjust up and down at least 5".

>> Use a stool or movable seat if necessary to rest your feet while you work on a client.

>> Raise your feet on a stool when you take a break.

>> Adjust facial stool and facial chair or bed up or down and make sure you are comfortable.

*Adapted from Health and Safety for Hair Care and Beauty Professionals, Labor Occupational Health Program, University of California at Berkeley.

Is it Time for New Shoes?

Rotating footwear makes shoes last longer, strengthens your arch and reduces fatigue. Here are a few suggestions from *Modern Salon* on when it's time to invest in a new pair:

1. You wear your work shoes on your days off.
2. All of your shoes are of the same type. You should have different shoes for different activities.
3. The shoes offer little or no arch support.
4. You don't have shoes that use new lightweight technology.
5. Your size has changed; sizes are good guidelines, but ultimately buy what feels comfortable.

HANDS AND WRISTS

Most of the muscles that move your hand and fingers are actually in your forearm. These muscles are connected to the hand and fingers by tendons, which are like cords passing through your wrist. **Tendonitis** occurs when the tendons get inflamed.

The carpal tunnel is a tunnel in the wrist, surrounded by bone and tissue. A nerve and several tendons pass through this tunnel. If you have tendonitis, the tendons swell and the nerve in the tunnel gets pinched. This condition, called **Carpal Tunnel Syndrome**, can make your hands numb and weak.

The main causes of tendonitis and Carpal Tunnel Syndrome are:

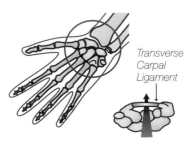

Transverse Carpal Ligament

Carpal Tunnel

1. Bending your wrist frequently

2. Pinching or gripping with force

3. Repeating a motion over and over

Tendonitis, Carpal Tunnel Syndrome and other hand/wrist problems can occur when you:

» Cut hair, hold a blow dryer or use a round brush, curlers or curling iron

» Cut with shears that don't fit your hand

» Cut with shears that are dull or not lubricated properly

» Apply perm rods or rollers

» Massage a client

» Use a comb that doesn't glide smoothly

DISCOVER**MORE**

For beauty professionals, using your arms and doing repeated movements with your hands and wrists are a big part of your daily job. When performing some of these activities, try alternating hands when possible, take frequent breaks and use the **RICE** home treatments:

Rest and protect injured or sore areas.

Ice the area to prevent or minimize swelling.

Compress or wrap injured areas with a bandage to help decrease swelling.

Elevate the injured area while applying ice and any time you are sitting or lying down.

Search online for more information.

General

>> Bend your wrists as little as possible when using your hands.

>> Use procedural techniques that help you keep your wrists straight.

>> Train your nondominant hand to do more tasks.

>> Perform regular hand exercises and self-massage your hands.

>> See a massage therapist periodically.

Service-Specific

>> Adjust the chair height—lower to work on the crown of the head and higher to work below ear level; swivel the chair so you don't have to reach over or across the client.

>> Try to position yourself next to your client so that you don't have to raise your arms.

>> Tilt the client's head so you don't have to bend your arm, hand and wrist as much.

>> Use sharp shears that fit your hand and are correctly adjusted/lubricated; fewer cuts and less force will be needed for each cut you make.

>> Twirl the handle of your round brush between your thumb and index finger instead of continually bending your wrist.

>> Use armrests for both you and the client at manicure stations.

>> Use the strength of your arms, not your hands and wrists, during massage; relax your hands when working on a client.

Adapted from Health and Safety for Hair Care and Beauty Professionals, Labor Occupational Health Program, University of California at Berkeley.

Hand Stretches

1. Place fingers on the edge of a table.

2. Push down gently, stretching the muscles of fingers.

3. Drop elbows and push again so that this time you are stretching the wrist muscles.

4. Repeat 3 times and hold for 3-4 seconds each.

5. Return hands to normal position, and then place thumbs on the edge of the table.

6. Push down gently, and roll your thumbs to the side to stretch the muscles of each side.

7. Hold hands straight out in front of you and clench your fists.

8. Rotate at the wrists 5 times in one direction, then 5 times in the other direction. ▐▐

Adapted from Free4m: The Holistic Approach to Hairdressing.

DISCOVER**MORE**

Manufacturers are doing their part to sustain the health and careers of salon professionals. For example, dryer brands have been making an effort to decrease weight, shorten drying times and allow for a pain-free grip. Some of the latest tool innovations include:

Ergonomic shears with adjustable finger rests to allow designers to drop their shoulders and use fewer hand and wrist movements

Automatic curling tools that reduce fatigue from manually turning traditional curling irons

Lightweight brushes with aluminum handles

SHOULDERS

Your shoulder has muscles and tendons. If you strain your shoulder, you can get muscle aches, tendonitis or **bursitis**—an inflammation of the fluid-filled sac (bursa) that lies between a tendon and skin or a tendon and bone. You risk straining your shoulder if you often hold your arm stretched away from your body, or up with your elbow above shoulder height.

You may strain your shoulder when you:

>> Reach up to cut, dry or curl the crown of the head

>> Reach across the client's body to shampoo or dry hair

>> Reach across a table to do manicures

>> Reach for shears and combs on the counter

>> Reach for supplies on a high shelf

>> Hold heavy clippers, especially if your arm is stretched out or raised

RECOMMENDATIONS TO PREVENT SHOULDER PROBLEMS

General

>> Do stretching and range-of-motion (ROM) exercises for your arms and shoulders.

>> Maintain good posture. Stand straight and relaxed, without slumping.

>> Don't lift or carry objects that are too heavy for you.

Service-Specific

>> Adjust the chair height and swivel the chair when you work on a client so your arms are close to your sides.

>> Tilt the client's head to a position that is comfortable for you.

>> Hold your tools so you don't have to raise your arms.

>> Use an armrest when you do a manicure or support your arms on folded towels.

>> Twirl the handle of your round brush between your thumb and index finger instead of continually bending your wrist.

>> Position facial chair or bed and facial machines to be close to you to avoid unnecessary reaching.

>> Be sure not to tense your shoulders while performing facial treatments and massage.

Adapted from Health and Safety for Hair Care and Beauty Professionals, Labor Occupational Health Program, University of California at Berkeley.

Shoulder and Arm Stretches

1. Extend your arms out to the side of your body.

2. Rotate arms forward 5 times, then backward 5 times.

3. Stand upright, twist your body at the waist as far as you can on one side. Then twist to the other side. Do each side 5 times.

4. Bend to one side at your waist, bringing your arm up over your head. Keep your other arm either beside or behind your waist. Then do the other side. Do each side 5 times.

Adapted from Free4m: The Holistic Approach to Hairdressing.

Being aware of your body movements, the position and types of equipment and tools you use will help you have a more comfortable, sustainable career in the beauty industry.

SALON**CONNECTION**

Ergonomic Recommendations for Estheticians and Nail Technicians

Although standing may seem like an easier option, performing facial treatments from a seated position is better for your body. The correct seated position—for skin and nail services alike—will allow you to perform client services with less strain on your feet, legs, shoulders and back.

» Help your client sit in the facial chair or bed and recline comfortably in a horizontal position.

» Take a seat at the head of the facial chair or bed, making sure the headrest is above your waist and below your chest.

» Sit with your back straight and both feet on the floor directly below your knees when performing facials or nail services.

» Pull in your stomach muscles to help support your back.

» Adjust the height of your treatment chair if you find your back, shoulders or arms are uncomfortable when you are trying to reach your client's face, shoulder or upper chest area during a facial.

» Adjust the height/position of your chair if you experience discomfort when trying to reach your client's hands or feet during services.

LESSONS LEARNED

>> Ergonomics is important because it can extend the longevity of your salon career. Ergonomics affects a salon professional's job performance by providing solutions to maintain health and comfort based on the study of how you work, your body movements and the tools and equipment you use.

>> Common causes of neck and back pain include activities such as bending forward, twisting your body, leaning back, reaching overhead and standing for long periods of time. Keeping your back straight, bending at the hips instead of the waist, sitting with your feet flat on the floor and performing stretching exercises will help prevent injury.

>> Common causes of foot and leg problems include standing for long periods of time, wearing high heels and/or pointed shoes and shoes that don't fit well. Changing positions frequently, resting your feet, wearing comfortable shoes and using cushioned floor mats will help prevent problems.

>> Common causes of hand and wrist problems such as tendonitis and Carpal Tunnel Syndrome include bending the wrists, gripping and pinching with force and repetitive hand movements. Bending your wrists as little as possible when using your hands and performing regular hand exercises and hand massages on yourself can prevent these problems.

>> Common causes of shoulder strain include reaching up and across clients or reaching for tools and supplies on high shelves. Stretching exercises, good posture and lifting only lightweight items will help prevent strain. //

101ᶜ.3 | BASIC COMMUNICATION

EXPLORE //

Has autocorrect ever created a misunderstanding between you and someone else?

INSPIRE //

Effective communicators make favorable impressions.

ACHIEVE //

Following this lesson on *Basic Communication*, you'll be able to:

>> Identify, monitor and use forms of nonverbal communication to your advantage

>> Express clear and concise verbal messages

>> Explain the elements of effective communication

>> Compare the key points of two-way communication

>> Examine strategies that result in good listening habits

FOCUS //

BASIC COMMUNICATION

Nonverbal Communication

Verbal Communication

Listening

101°.3 BASIC COMMUNICATION

Take a look at the images below. What kind of message is each person sending?

Communication involves more than using your mouth to speak and your ears to listen. Your tone of voice, facial expressions, hand gestures, the words you choose and the questions you ask all play a part. Every time you exchange ideas, thoughts or feelings with someone, you are communicating. Your communication skills are just as important to your success as your technical skills.

NONVERBAL COMMUNICATION

In **nonverbal communication**, sometimes called body language, messages are exchanged without speaking. For example:

BODY LANGUAGE	MESSAGE
Smiling	Universal sign of approval
Standing straight, shoulders squared, head held high and extending a hand to greet	Communicates self-confidence
Bowed shoulders and sloping body posture	Conveys uncertainty
Eye contact, letting the speaker know they have your full attention	Universal sign of acknowledgement

SALON**CONNECTION**

Communicating With the Client

Imagine two hair designers, David and Leanne, who are each trying to convince a client that a shorter haircut will be more flattering than a shoulder-length style. David and Leanne are using exactly the same words to describe the look they have in mind. But David is standing straight and tall, facing his client directly, smiling, making eye contact and using hand gestures around the face as he describes the hairstyle. Leanne, on the other hand, is standing with her shoulders hunched, one shoulder turned toward the client and the other toward the mirror, biting her lower lip, shifting her gaze between the client's face and the floor, and wringing her hands while she speaks. Which hair designer is communicating with more confidence? Whose client will be more likely to take their designer's advice?

First impressions are often formed before a single word is uttered. Review the elements of body language in the following chart and think about how nonverbal communication supports and strengthens your messages, or how it may be working against you.

ELEMENTS OF NONVERBAL COMMUNICATION

KEY ELEMENTS	RECOMMENDATIONS
Facial Expression Gesture, look or aspect of the face	>> Offer a genuine smile to everyone you meet and greet >> Pay attention to what your facial expression is saying >> Avoid negative facial expressions such as a furrowed brow, frowning or twisting your lips to one side
Eye Contact Direct gaze of two people looking into one another's eyes	>> Make eye contact as soon as you start a conversation; use it earlier if you want to gain the person's attention >> Use eye contact throughout the conversation to communicate interest; avoid prolonged staring into another person's eyes >> Avoid looking over the other person's shoulders as though you find someone or something else more interesting
Gesture Body movement or mannerism	>> Use a firm, steady handshake >> Express confidence by keeping your hands out of your pockets; avoid fidgeting >> Nod occasionally to affirm you are listening >> Avoid gestures that could be considered negative such as clock-watching, finger or foot-tapping, pointing or shaking your finger or crossing your arms over your chest
Posture Carriage, position or stance of the body	>> Position yourself with stomach in, chest out, shoulders back, head up and plant your feet about 6-8" apart; stand or sit with a straight back; avoid slouching >> Lean forward to communicate, "I'm interested in what you are saying." Leaning away might say, "I've had enough."
Proximity Nearness of another to one's personal space	>> Avoid positioning yourself too closely, which comes across as pushy or threatening >> Avoid positioning yourself too far away, which comes across as distant or standoffish

VERBAL COMMUNICATION

How you speak is as important as what you're saying. As you use words to convey thoughts and information, try to express yourself in a way others can clearly understand.

Verbal communication can also influence the meaning of what you say. **The tone or inflection of your voice, level and rate of speech all play an important role in verbal communication.** The following is a 3-step approach to speaking with clarity:

1. Less is more.

2. Get to the point.

3. Focus on what's important.

DISCOVER**MORE**

Common Speaking Mistakes

WENT versus GONE
Incorrect: "I have went there before."
Correct: "I have gone there before."
Incorrect: "He gone home."
Correct: "He went home."
Both are forms of the verb *to go*; *went* is the past tense; *gone* is the past participle and follows has, had or have.

OF versus HAVE
Incorrect: "I would of been on time."
Correct: "I would have been on time."
Many people use poor enunciation when saying *have* so that it sounds like *of*.

CAN versus MAY
Incorrect: "How can I help you?"
Correct: "How may I help you?"
Incorrect: "Can I shampoo you now?"
Correct: "May I shampoo you now?"
Can suggests ability. *May* suggests permission.

GOOD versus WELL
Incorrect: "This shampoo works good on dry hair."
Correct: "This shampoo works well on dry hair."
Correct: "This is a good shampoo for your hair."
Good is an adjective. *Well* is usually an adverb.

ELEMENTS OF EFFECTIVE VERBAL COMMUNICATION

KEY ELEMENTS	RECOMMENDATIONS
Clarity Characterized by precision of language and clearness in the voice	>> Use proper **enunciation** (pronouncing words clearly, precisely and accurately); avoid dropping the ends of words or sentences and running words together >> Be specific with your word choices; refrain from using excess words or phrases that cause confusion such as "sort of," "a lot," "more or less" and "you know what I mean" >> Be prepared to speak; avoid muffled and/or hesitant speech such as starting every sentence with "uh" or "umm" or finishing sentences with "ya know" >> Avoid chewing gum, giggling or frequently clearing your throat/nose while speaking
Appropriate Vocabulary Use of acceptable expressions, terms and words	>> Use words that create a clear mental picture >> Recognize and avoid common grammar mistakes such as double negatives (i.e. hardly never) and ending sentences with prepositions (i.e. Where's the bathroom at?) >> Don't use derogatory, profane or politically motivated expressions; avoid slang or jargon
Pitch Tone and frequency used in communication; high or low vocal tones	>> Use **inflection,** vary your tone of voice when speaking; avoid extremes such as monotone and high pitch >> Match the tone of your voice to what you want to convey
Rate Tempo used during a verbal exchange; the quickness or slowness of your speech	>> Vary the rate you speak to maintain attention >> Speak slowly when explaining difficult concepts
Force Strength of volume used during a verbal exchange; from soft to loud	>> Speak loud enough to be easily heard, but not so loud that others feel you're shouting >> Pay attention to environmental factors such as the size of the room and background noise
Questioning Statements used to encourage a response from another person	>> Open-ended questions encourage a response beyond "yes" or "no" and usually begin with Who, What, Why, Where, When or How *Example: "What made you unhappy with your past salon visits?"* >> Closed-ended questions are usually answered with "yes" or "no" and often begin with Would, Do, Did, Could or May *Example: "Do you like the fragrance of this product?"*

> People you interact with expect you to use language that clearly communicates your thoughts, needs and ideas.

GRAMMAR

If language is not used correctly, your level of communication and understanding can be impaired.

Using poor grammar can begin accidentally when you copy poor speech patterns heard around you–perhaps to create a certain effect or for emphasis. This could easily impact your recognition as a professional.

TWO-WAY COMMUNICATION

In the salon industry, the line between social and professional communication is not always clear-cut. Language that may be acceptable among your friends and family is not always appropriate in the workplace. Here are several points to improve your two-way communication skills:

PRESENT A PLEASANT GREETING

>> Always greet a client using the last name (Mrs. Brown, Mr. Smith, Ms. Johnson) unless the client offers permission to use their first name.

>> Use a pleasant tone of voice that projects eagerness in offering your services.

USE TACT

>> **Tact** is learning to say the proper thing without offending someone. This skill requires sensitivity and diplomacy.

>> It's your responsibility to communicate honestly with clients, without offending them.

>> Think an idea through completely before you talk about it.

KNOW THE PURPOSE AND IMPORTANCE OF YOUR IDEAS

>> Is your purpose to gain information, change an attitude, seek support, and/or motivate?

>> Consider the listener's needs and desires to qualify the purpose and importance of your comments.

>> Ask yourself: How will the listener benefit from what I'm saying?

>> Be prepared to show your ideas visually to support what is being suggested to the client.

BE AWARE OF YOUR ENVIRONMENT

>> Be sure the timing is right for your communication.

>> Be discreet; decide whether your ideas or feelings should be expressed in public or private.

>> Consider who should hear your thoughts, ideas and feelings.

WATCH YOUR OVERTONES

>> An overtone occurs when your tone of voice, inflection, expressions and reactions do not match your words. Example: You saying, "I'm so happy to see you today," without smiling or extending your hand in greeting.

>> Be sure you are communicating the idea you want to convey.

CONSULT WITH OTHERS WHEN NECESSARY

>> Be certain you have all the facts and information available.

>> If you're in doubt, consult with others to gain new insights, ideas, opinions and support.

>> Concentrate on understanding others first.

>> Listening is an important key to good communication.

Language that may be acceptable among your friends and family is not always appropriate in the workplace.

LISTENING

Listening well is just as important as speaking well, and it's not just a matter of being quiet. Being a good listener means knowing how to focus your attention on the speaker and what is being said.

ELEMENTS OF GOOD LISTENING HABITS

KEY ELEMENTS	RECOMMENDATIONS
Focus Attention Be aware and informed of what is going on around you	>> Maintain open listening; avoid prejudging >> Be authentic; ask questions to show sincere interest >> Pay attention to nonverbal messages; notice body language and major ideas communicated >> Listen all the way to the end; don't assume you know the ending >> Understand that listening is not waiting for your turn to speak >> Recognize that listening requires intention and energy; avoid an in-and-out listening pattern; be present in the moment
Respond Acknowledge or clarify communication	>> Reply to the speaker to affirm you are listening >> Remain silent to give the speaker time to breathe and think; then prompt if necessary >> Offer periodic comments such as "go on" or "tell me more" to prompt the speaker to continue
Repeat Verify communication by restating	>> Restate what you heard to verify message >> Listen for details and repeat factual information to gain accuracy
Paraphrase Translate what you heard into your own words	>> Show your understanding by putting the other person's thoughts into your own words >> Summarize the meaning of what has been communicated
Question Expand, clarify and confirm your understanding by questioning	>> Ask open-ended questions to gain additional information so you fully understand what's being said >> Ask closed-ended questions to verify that you have understood accurately

A good communicator knows how to make a favorable impression on people, and this can help make you a respected salon professional.

LESSONS LEARNED

›› Appropriate forms of nonverbal communication that can be used to your advantage when communicating include facial expressions, eye contact, gestures, posture and proximity.

›› Elements of clear and concise verbal communication include clarity, appropriate vocabulary, pitch, rate, force and questioning.

›› Effective communication includes verbal and nonverbal elements such as:

Facial Expressions   Gestures

                                                    Proximity

Inflection   Level and Rate of Speech

Eye Contact   Posture   Grammar

›› Key points that can be compared for improving two-way communication include:
- Present a pleasant greeting
- Use tact
- Recognize the purpose and importance of the ideas being communicated
- Be aware of your environment
- Watch overtones
- Consult with others when necessary

›› Elements of good listening habits include focusing attention, responding, repeating, paraphrasing and questioning.

101ᶜ.4 | COMMUNICATE WITH CONFIDENCE

EXPLORE //

What does "a little off the top" mean to you? Do you think it means the same thing to your hairstylist?

INSPIRE //

Your success in communicating with your clients is strongly related to how well you do as a professional.

ACHIEVE //

Following this lesson on *Communicate With Confidence*, you'll be able to:

>> List flexing strategies that will ensure others understand you

>> Apply professional etiquette to show respect, integrity and commitment to personal excellence

>> Practice guidelines for communication challenges

>> Offer ways to solve scheduling issues while maintaining good client relationships

FOCUS //

COMMUNICATE WITH CONFIDENCE

Communication Essentials

Interacting With Clients

101ᶜ.4
COMMUNICATE WITH CONFIDENCE

Have you ever stopped at the store for one single item, but after a few minutes with a sales associate you're at the counter with a basket of products? Engaging you in conversation, listening to your wants/needs and offering an agreeable solution likely helped the associate make that sale. Your ability to communicate effectively with your clients will help you reach your goals throughout your career in the beauty industry.

COMMUNICATION ESSENTIALS

Clearly understanding and interpreting client requests will help you provide the exact service they desire.

The best way to do this is:

1. Encourage them to give you enough information to understand their desires.

2. Be a good listener and ask questions if necessary.

3. Practice reflective listening by paraphrasing what has been communicated.

The best speakers realize that communication is a two-way street and are able to flex during the course of a conversation. **Flexing** means adjusting your behavior to ensure that your messages are being understood, and adapting your approach as needed. Some flexing strategies you can use when speaking include:

1. Tuning in to how others are most comfortable interacting

2. Finding things in common with others

3. Showing concern and compassion

4. Using questions to show interest and increase your understanding

The topics you select to discuss with your clients should be chosen with care. **Avoid controversial topics during client discussions:**

>> Religion
>> Politics
>> Personal problems
>> Other clients' behavior
>> Workmanship of other staff or competitors
>> Information given to you in confidence

As a salon professional, you'll want to focus your conversation on your client's lifestyle and salon-related needs, and then completely focus on your client's home care needs.

SALON**CONNECTION**

Conversation Icebreakers

General Topics:
>> How do you like the weather we've been having?
>> Did you run into much traffic on the way to the salon?
>> Have you tried the new restaurant downtown?
>> Did you see the game last night?

Work Topics:
>> What kind of work do you do?
>> I'm not familiar with that type of work. Can you tell me more about it?
>> What's new in your industry/line of work?
>> Has the economy had much effect on your business?

Personal Topics:
>> What's new with you?
>> What do you do for fun?
>> Do you have any special plans for the weekend?
>> What's new with your family?

Salon Topics:
>> Your look is classic/fun/natural.
>> How much time do you like to spend on your hair/skin/nails?
>> What haven't you liked about your previous hair/skin/nail care?
>> What would you like to accomplish today during your visit to the salon?

INTERACTING WITH CLIENTS

Good manners translate everywhere. In the workplace, practicing good manners is referred to as professional etiquette. Professional etiquette helps define your character and confirms a certain level of respect, integrity and commitment to your craft. Professional etiquette will always be noticed and appreciated by those around you.

PROFESSIONAL ETIQUETTE

RESPECT

» Use respectful language such as "please," "thank you," "hello," "goodbye," "good morning" and "excuse me."

» Introduce yourself and others; ask people for the correct pronunciation of their names.

» Be helpful; open doors regardless of gender.

» Listen with interest.

» Refrain from loud verbal exchanges.

» Offer praise and compliments generously but sincerely; receive praise and compliments graciously.

» Write thank-you notes promptly; respond to emails and phone messages within 24 hours.

» Limit mobile phone use to personal time.

» Avoid stereotyping; do not make assumptions about people based on appearances.

INTEGRITY

» Apologize when you make a mistake or inconvenience others; express regret for accidents.

» Avoid exaggerating and inflating the truth.

» Choose the right time and place to discuss business and personal matters.

» Say "no" in a tactful way when responding to a request you cannot perform; offer alternative solutions.

» Communicate in open, honest ways; discuss appropriate topics.

» Do what you say you will—match your actions with your words.

» Support the success of others.

» Do the right thing regardless of the personal inconvenience.

» Take responsibility for your actions

COMMITMENT

» Display a professional appearance and friendly, enthusiastic personality.

» Honor time schedules; prepare and arrive on time for work, appointments and meetings.

» Be dedicated to helping clients achieve the results they want.

» Establish professional goals.

» Stay informed about industry trends.

» Engage in lifelong learning.

» Represent the profession through involvement in the community.

» Persevere through difficult times.

DISCOVER**MORE**

To avoid placing blame or sounding accusatory, try using "I" statements and think about how you will say something before you speak to a co-worker. Instead of: "You need to clean this work area today," try, "I know we all agreed to take turns cleaning this area and I see it is your turn today. Do you need any help?"

COMMUNICATION CHALLENGES

Like most workplaces, conflicts can happen in the salon. With some basic communication techniques for problem-solving and conflict resolution, they can be managed effectively.

GUIDELINES FOR HANDLING COMMUNICATION CHALLENGES

Stay in Control of Your Emotions	» Stay calm. » Don't take client comments personally—even if they sound personal. » Realize that if clients lash out at you, it is likely the result of something unrelated that happened before your interaction with them.
Stay Open	» Try not to prejudge the situation, interrogate the client or tell them not to be angry or upset. » Convey to the client that you are not interested in being right or proving your point, but in finding a mutually agreeable solution. » Remain warm and approachable.
Stay Positive	» Be confident that together, you and your client will find a workable solution. » Stay respectful of yourself and your client. » Avoid placing blame by using the "I versus You" technique.
Stay Focused	» Address one issue at a time. » As soon as you notice the discussion getting off-track, bring it back to the main issue.

SCHEDULING CONCERNS

While working in the salon you may be faced with issues such as clients arriving late, clients arriving early, clients who fail to show up for their appointment and other scheduling mix-ups. Maintaining client relationships is what it's all about. Here are some quick ways to help address these scheduling concerns.

LATE CLIENTS

» Remind client of scheduled service time, and ask if there was difficulty getting to the salon.

» Explain what services you have time to complete.

» Discuss issue after the service in a private setting.

EARLY CLIENTS

» Welcome client warmly.

» Tell client how long before service will begin.

» Provide reading material and beverage.

NO-SHOW CLIENTS

» Make reminder call ahead of time.

» Call client to discuss missed appointment.

» Inform client of cancellation policy, if appropriate.

» Offer to reschedule appointment.

SCHEDULING MIX-UPS

» Obtain all information about appointment you can from client.

» Ask client to give you a moment to investigate the situation.

» Apologize to client for any inconvenience.

» Alert management if you are unable to correct the situation.

When communicating with clients, take the time to ask questions and encourage them to express their opinions. Good communication skills will go a long way toward helping you become a successful salon professional.

LESSONS LEARNED

>> Flexing strategies include tuning in to how others are most comfortable interacting, finding things in common, showing concern and compassion, and demonstrating interest by asking questions.

>> Modeling respect, integrity and commitment are important steps in modeling professional etiquette.

>> Some guidelines for handling communication challenges include:

- Staying in control of emotions
- Staying open
- Staying positive
- Staying focused

>> Maintaining good client relationships includes being able to solve scheduling issues related to late clients, early clients, no-show clients and scheduling mix-ups.

101ᶜ.5 | HUMAN RELATIONS

EXPLORE //

What would the world be like if there were no relationships at all?

"We don't get harmony when everybody sings the same note. Only notes that are different can harmonize. The same is true with people."

—Steve Goodier

INSPIRE //

Getting along with others helps
you in everything you do.

ACHIEVE //

Following this lesson on *Human
Relations*, you'll be able to:

>> Point out the role personality, attitude
and habits play in human relations

>> Compare respect, self-respect, self-
esteem and mutual respect

>> Explain the meaning of professional ethics

FOCUS //

HUMAN RELATIONS

Personality

Respect

Ethics

101°.5 HUMAN RELATIONS

Have you ever had a hard time getting along with someone? Chances are, you have. The psychology of getting along with others is referred to as **human relations**. Many factors influence good human relations in the workplace, including personality, respect and your professional code of ethics. Long hours of standing, high client expectations and the need to increase your work pace can cause added stress. Be sure that this stress doesn't negatively reflect in how you deal with people.

PERSONALITY

Personality is defined as the outward reflection of your inner feelings, thoughts, attitudes and values. Your individual personality consists of combinations of many different human characteristics, such as:

>> Emotions
>> Attitudes
>> Skills
>> Beliefs
>> Values
>> Goals

All of your experiences influence the development of your personality, too. These personality characteristics are not quickly changed, but can be modified over time.

ATTITUDES

An **attitude** is the specific and identifiable emotion and/or reaction one experiences and projects in dealing with the demands of life. Because your attitude is projected, it can have an effect on those around you. A negative attitude, obviously, can have a negative impact on others. Projecting a positive attitude can have an uplifting effect on the people around you. Attitudes can be changed.

"Positive" and "negative" are the two words that typically describe attitudes. Other

descriptions include (but aren't limited to):

>> Enthusiastic
>> Caring
>> Confident
>> Defensive
>> Aggressive
>> Fearful

An attractive personality, including a positive attitude, is one of your greatest

assets in life. The effect you have on other people is the charm revealed in your speech, appearance, behavior and manner. If you develop and nurture a positive attitude, you'll make clients feel good in your presence, and you'll be able to help them look good and feel great.

HABITS

Some people bite their nails, others bite their lips. Some people drum their fingers, others tap their feet. The only thing all these actions have in common is that the people performing them are probably not aware of doing so. These actions are very likely all habits.

Habits are defined as a routine of behavior that is repeated regularly and tends to occur unconsciously. A few notes to remember about habits:

>> They are learned and reinforced through events in your environment, which strengthen them.

>> Most habits are harmless actions that others barely notice.

>> Some ingrained habits are annoying.

You're entering a service business and can benefit from toning down or eliminating those habits others may find annoying, as they can limit your potential for success.

Having a positive attitude and practicing good habits are two keys to getting along with people.

Be Courteous

>> **Courtesy** is polite behavior that shows respect for other people.

>> Courtesy helps clients feel comfortable and relaxed with you.

>> Manage your personal and professional schedule to avoid conflicts with time.

>> Arrive at work on time. Fifteen minutes prior to starting time is preferred by most employers. //

DISCOVER**MORE**

You can learn how to break bad habits and build positive ones. The first step is monitoring them. Make a well-considered list of all your habits. Review each item on your list. Is each habit consistent with the personal image you want to present to others? If not, begin a program of change now. Many apps are available online to help track your progress.

RESPECT

Respect is a feeling of deep admiration for someone or something.

>> Respect that people have for themselves is called **self-respect**.

>> Respect that people have for one another is **mutual respect.**

SELF-RESPECT

Have you ever been asked to do something that made you uncomfortable or that you knew would hurt someone else? Speaking up about your feelings in situations like this is a sign of self-respect. Think of **self-respect** as pride in yourself and the assurance that you are behaving with honor and dignity. You simply feel better about yourself and your ability.

A person with self-respect likes him or herself. Through a process of self-examination and self-improvement, you actually are choosing to become your own best friend. Paying attention to what you like about yourself can help build self-respect.

People who build self-respect:

>> Feel better about themselves, others and life in general
>> Seek out other positive people
>> Resist negative influences and steer clear of those who are stuck in negativity
>> Expect, accept and embrace change
>> Make the best of the positives in people and situations

Self-esteem is confidence and satisfaction in oneself. As a form of respect, self-esteem helps maintain a good sense of self, and this helps with others. Self-esteem is a powerful motivator that encourages us to improve ourselves and work in positive, productive ways.

Achieving or maintaining high self-esteem is a lifelong process. It's normal to have days when you don't want to deal with personal challenges. But allowing these feelings to rule and prevent you from connecting positively with others isn't in your best interest. If you want to build positive self-esteem, pick something that you enjoy, and perfect it to the best of your ability.

POSITIVE SELF-ESTEEM IN ACTION

This person:

» Shows resilience in the face of adversity

» Smiles a lot; has positive beliefs about family/society

» Displays lots of energy; sets and accomplishes goals

» Forms long-term friendships

» Looks others in the eye and acts with confidence

» Accepts risks; acts immediately

» Demonstrates optimism

» Tells the truth and keeps commitments

NEGATIVE SELF-ESTEEM IN ACTION

This person:

» Fears adversity and authority figures

» Smiles rarely; holds limiting beliefs

» Tires quickly; avoids setting goals

» Tends to isolate from others

» Avoids eye contact with others

» Avoids risks

» Demonstrates pessimism

» Bends the truth and doesn't keep commitments

DISCOVER**MORE**

You'll be working closely with clients in a service business, so a healthy self-esteem is beneficial in many ways. There are plenty of ways to build self-esteem. Try searching online for the top 5 or 10 ways to build self-esteem.

Self-confidence is the best outfit, rock it and own it.

SALON**CONNECTION**

R-E-S-P-E-C-T Chart

QUALITY AND ACTION	RELATIONSHIP TO CAREER: A successful professional...
Reliability Fulfills obligations	» Shows up for work on time as assigned » Calls the employer if not able to come to work » Does the best work possible » Accepts accountability for expected results, goals and client satisfaction
Enthusiasm Cultivates an optimistic and energetic disposition	» Smiles and displays an upbeat attitude » Shows interest in clients, co-workers and the profession » Displays a personal warmth that is attractive to others
Sincerity Acts authentically to benefit others and self	» Promotes honesty with clients, co-workers and self » Follows through on commitments » Acts and speaks with day-to-day consistency
Persistence Turns setbacks into comebacks	» Provides client satisfaction, even in stressful situations » Offers retail, additional services and future appointments on an ongoing basis » Exhibits resilience; bounces back from mistakes
Emotional Balance Becomes more aware of and controls emotions	» Responds calmly versus reacts impulsively; thinks before acting » Maintains a healthy physical condition to support energy level and stamina » Is polite, respectful and appropriate » Identifies problems and offers solutions
Consideration Considers the feelings and needs of others	» Makes adjustments based on client and co-worker needs and situations, from simple to complex, such as celebrations, illnesses or funerals » Displays a willingness to be flexible
Trustworthiness Tells the truth even when it is unpopular to do so	» Handles money, hours, equipment and pressure in an honest manner » Informs management of issues that need to be resolved

Emotional balance, or self-control, is learned behavior that doesn't always happen naturally. A successful professional keeps emotions in check in the workplace. Achieving emotional balance when working in the salon industry is especially important because it is a rapidly changing profession that involves constant interaction with clients and co-workers.

MUTUAL RESPECT

Mutual respect, the respect that two people have for one another, feeds each person's need to feel valued.

How does mutual respect show up in the workplace? You don't have to like everyone you work with to respect them. Even though your co-workers may not be your best friends, if you show them respect, they will usually reflect it back to you. Mutual respect helps create a positive and productive environment.

> Building mutual respect at work will often require you to take the first step. You can't control how other people behave and whether they show respect or not, but you can take responsibility for your actions. Sometimes this means showing respect first.

Here's an easy way to grasp the elements of respect.

EXAMPLES OF RESPECT

Self-Respect

"I like myself. I have qualities and personal traits that I respect in myself and others, such as strength of character, integrity, dedication, generosity and steadfastness." This list will be different for every person.

Self-Esteem

"I believe in myself and in my ability to make my way in the world."

Mutual Respect

"I have the confidence to live authentically and to recognize and appreciate the positive qualities of others. I demonstrate my respect for others and others respect me in return."

Four Strategies to Demonstrate Respect at Work

Practicing these strategies and making them part of your natural way of doing things will build mutual respect in the workplace. It will also result in earning respect from your peers, your supervisors and your clients.

1. **Be courteous**.

   Most people know the rules of common courtesy. It's amazing how far a simple "please," "thank you," "excuse me" and "I'm sorry" can go.

2. **Be considerate** of other people's likes and dislikes.

   People bring many different personal preferences to the workplace, and it's only natural to want to get your way whenever possible. What do you do when your "like" bumps up against someone else's "dislike"? Think about what's really important to you and what's important to those around you, and make allowances when you can.

3. **Be sensitive** to other people's feelings.

   When people are stressed or facing difficult circumstances, they may not behave in rational or likeable ways. Take extra care with what you say and do to help others preserve their own dignity and self-respect.

4. **Be interested** in other people's thoughts and opinions.

   The highest respect a person can show another is to listen and be interested to what others have to say. Ask questions to get a deeper understanding. Try not to be defensive when others have different views. You can value differences of opinion without losing your own point of view.

MUTUAL RESPECT DO'S AND DON'TS

DO	DON'T
Do look at people when talking to them and when they're talking to you.	Don't get distracted or let your eyes wander.
Do compliment others for good work or effort and risk-taking.	Don't withhold praise in order to feel superior.
Do send thank-you notes.	Don't take the kindness of others for granted.
Do smile at others.	Don't wait for others to smile at you.
Do respect other people's time and keep your commitments.	Don't act as if everyone's schedule revolves around you; don't assume that nobody notices when you don't follow through.
Do open doors for others, especially for people who are weak or have their hands full.	Don't assume that opening doors is old-fashioned or sexist.
Do use appropriate, respectful language.	Don't assume that foul language is "cool" or acceptable.
Do give your full attention to the task and people at hand.	Don't leave your phone on, make calls or send texts unless necessary for vital communication.
Do maintain a professional appearance, and assess every work situation and the effect of your behavior on others.	Don't dress provocatively or wear strong fragrances, and don't eat or chew gum in most work settings, especially when speaking.

SALON**CONNECTION**

Mutual Respect Builds Teamwork

Creating a harmonious salon environment depends heavily on teamwork. As a member of a team, you can have a positive influence on the group. Strong, positive, professional relationships and team spirit take time to build. You can begin by establishing rapport with each person and working toward good communication, understanding and teamwork every day. Following are some tips on teamwork in the salon:

>> Keep your workstation clean with all your tools in place.
>> Place and store salon tools after each use to help avoid frustration.
>> Respect confidences shared by peers or clients; this is essential to cultivating an atmosphere of trust and sharing.

If you're considerate and cooperative, you'll add to your team's success. //

ETHICS

As you grow older, you begin learning what is right or wrong. As your personality develops, you establish your own personal system of moral principles and values. This system guides you and is your personal ethics compass.

Your personal ethics carry over into your profession. **Professional ethics** deal with proper conduct in relationships with your employer, co-workers and clients.

Most professions have associations that establish a code of professional ethics for their individual members. It is important for you to familiarize yourself with the cosmetology code of ethics in your area.

Some of the responsibilities and ethics that will help you to build solid professional relationships with your clients and co-workers are listed on the sample professional code of ethics.

Sample Professional Code of Ethics

>> Show respect for the feelings and rights of others.

>> Be fair and courteous to your co-workers. Don't attempt to win clients away from them.

>> Be fair and courteous to your clients. Be consistent in pricing your services. Don't show favoritism to certain clients.

>> Be eager to learn new methods and techniques. Attend educational programs that provide updated information or help you improve your skills.

>> Represent yourself, your services and products honestly to the public. Do not advertise a service you cannot perform.

>> Set an example of good conduct and good behavior. Always cherish a good reputation.

>> Demonstrate loyalty to your employer and co-workers.

>> Keep your word and fulfill your obligations. Never break the confidence entrusted to you by a client or co-worker.

>> Practice only the highest standards of infection control as provided by your regulating agency laws. Keep your work area and tools spotlessly clean.

>> Believe in and be proud of your profession, just as you believe in yourself.

Commitment to Excellence

Invest in yourself. Learn everything you can in school. Take an active part in school activities. Take advantage of advanced education and seminars. After graduation, continue to invest in your education by attending seminars, shows and workshops. Be a lifelong learner. Keep pace with what's happening in the industry. Become known for your willingness to share your knowledge and your enthusiasm for the salon industry. There is no limit to the success you can achieve if you are willing to invest the time and energy success demands of the true professional.

Getting along with others is as much of a skill as your technical skills. The salon world is filled with creative, colorful personalities that you'll encounter throughout your career. Learning to navigate these relationships successfully will help you in everything you do—and not just the salon.

LESSONS LEARNED

>> Personality, attitude and habits play an important role in human relations because they are behaviors that can be projected outward to other people.

>> Respect is a feeling of deep admiration for someone or something and is based on positive traits such as reliability, enthusiasm, sincerity, persistence, emotional balance, consideration and trustworthiness. Self-respect is respect that people have for themselves. Self-esteem is confidence and satisfaction in oneself. Mutual respect is respect people have for one another.

>> Professional ethics deal with proper conduct in relationships with your employer, co-workers and clients.

EXPLORE //

Who is your role model?
Have you ever wondered
how to become that person?

INSPIRE //

Your success depends on daily choices that build resilience.

ACHIEVE //

Following this lesson on *Resilience*, you'll be able to:

>> Express what it means to have integrity

>> List behaviors that destroy trust in work relationships

>> Describe the value of making good life choices

>> Explain how resilience plays a role in your professional career

FOCUS //

RESILIENCE

Integrity

Commitment

▪101ᶜ.6 re·sil·ience

\ri- zil-y n(t)s\
noun

1. The ability of a substance or object to spring back in to shape; elasticity.
   "nylon is excellent in wearability and resilience"

2. The capacity to recover quickly from difficulties; toughness.
   "the often remarkable resilience of so many dedicated individuals"

Resilience is all about making mistakes and bouncing back. It's being able to pick yourself up, dust yourself off and move on! Integrity and commitment can help you build your resilience.

INTEGRITY

Do you know someone who avoids gossip, isn't secretive and matches their words and actions? Are you able to trust them no matter what? **Integrity** means being honest and having moral principles.

» It's doing the right thing, even when it is difficult and no one can see you.

» It's also doing what you say you will—not acting ethically only when it suits you.

"The greatest glory in living lies not in never falling, but in rising every time we fall."

—Nelson Mandela

"
Integrity is doing the right thing, even when no one is watching. "

—C.S. Lewis

Integrity doesn't require talent, brains, education or training; it's about the choices you make to build character. Good character is a safeguard against lapses that can destroy a career.

>> Character counts when it comes to personal success; it's a part of professional success.

>> You can't choose your parents or the circumstances you were born into.

>> But you can choose to develop your character into who you want to be.

"The time is always right to do what is right."
—Dr. Martin Luther King, Jr.

TRUST

Trust is the ability to create relationships built upon mutual respect and openness. Trusting others, especially at work, means going beyond self-interest and treating each other with respect and honesty.

>> In an atmosphere of trust, people are more relaxed and natural.

>> It's an environment where co-workers help each other and go beyond job expectations.

FIVE MOST EFFECTIVE WAYS TO BUILD OR LOSE TRUST AT WORK

	Build Trust	Lose Trust
1.	Stick to standards of ethical behavior	Tell half-truths
2.	Communicate in open, honest ways	Seek personal gain above shared gain
3.	Show respect for the ideas and beliefs of others	Withhold important information
4.	Focus on shared, mutually beneficial goals	Be closed to the ideas of others
5.	Do the right thing regardless of personal risk	Act inconsistently

Trust-Busters

Trust-busters diminish trust in the workplace. Example trust-busters include gossip, insincerity, inconsistency, poor work ethic, self-absorbed behavior and a lack of courage. In the following chart, each trust-buster has a sample response that could help defuse a situation at work.

TRUST-BUSTERS

GOSSIP
"I'm not comfortable listening to any more comments about Julie—she's not here to defend herself."

INSINCERITY
"I don't think you mean to sound like you don't care about anything around here, because I know you care about all of us."

INCONSISTENCY
"Yesterday you loved working here and today you're acting like you could pick up and leave anytime. What's up?"

POOR WORK ETHIC
"I just heard you say you weren't going to work. Didn't you promise to work the extra shift for Susan?"

SELF-ABSORBED BEHAVIOR
"Were you really thinking about what that client wanted? I heard her say she wanted to relax and you kept talking to her or the client next to you during the entire service."

LACK OF COURAGE
"What do you mean you want to quit? You can't give up now! You've worked too hard to give up!"

LIFE CHOICES

Every day we make choices about who we are and who we will become. Our choices shape the events of our lives, show our character and create our future.

» Choose trust and integrity and you open up your career to exciting possibilities.

» Choose insincerity and a poor work ethic, and life can become difficult and less fulfilling.

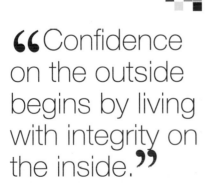

"Confidence on the outside begins by living with integrity on the inside."

—Brian Tracy

SALON**CONNECTION**

Salons Against Domestic Abuse

Domestic Violence

Salon professionals are in a unique position to recognize the signs and symptoms of abuse in their clients and co-workers. Because of the intimate and nurturing nature of the relationship between salon professionals and their clients and co-workers, salon professionals can often spot signs of physical abuse that others may never see.

Research shows that most battered women never call the police or go to a shelter.

However, they do usually talk about the abuse with someone they trust. Because salon professionals are skilled and experienced listeners who are personally interested in those around them, many victims suffering from abuse feel comfortable confiding in them— even if they would never tell anyone else. For an abused woman, the salon may be an ideal environment to seek out help because it may be one of the few places she is allowed to go without her abuser.

With proper training on how to recognize the signs of abuse and safely refer victims to help, salon professionals can become invaluable and influential community partners in the fight against domestic abuse.

Visit this website for additional information:
probeauty.org/cutitout/

LIFE CHOICES (CONT'D)

Abusing your health by using drugs and/or alcohol, and hanging out with people of questionable character, and/or staying in an abusive relationship aren't good life choices. Anything that diminishes self-respect or personal integrity is a questionable choice.

You've probably heard, "You are the company you keep." Your choice of friends is an important life choice. They influence your values, language, goals and how you spend your time.

BLIND SPOTS

Blind spots are negative aspects of ourselves that we're unaware of, but others can see. Blind spots that go uncorrected can create problems and limit success. Think about the following questions:

» Has anyone talked to you about a blind spot you have?

» Do you know anyone who has a blind spot regarding honesty, dependability, persistence or flexibility?

» Can you think of someone who was limited by a blind spot?

Being aware of our limitations is the beginning of personal improvement and growth.

"It's choice—not chance—that determines your destiny."

—Jean Nidetch

COMMITMENT

Commitment is a pledge to a course of action. Passion and commitment bring meaning and inspiration to your work, and provide the motivation and energy for you to go above and beyond. There are many people who succeeded despite what critics said; it took commitment and personal strength to see things through.

NEW CHALLENGES

A person who lives life fully directs energy and focused attention to their goals in ways that help to create the lives they want. This person also strives to learn new ways to handle problems and uses what's inside to lead a vigorous, productive, enjoyable life outside.

You'll often face new challenges, especially in the ever-changing industry you have chosen. Product innovations, new fashion trends and/or unpredictable market demands are common. Facing these new challenges with confidence and optimism gets you where you want to go.

Decide for Yourself

›› What are my personal strengths, talents and gifts?
›› When am I at my best?
›› Who is my best source of inspiration?
›› What are my most important goals right now?

❝Obstacles are what we see when we take our eyes off our goal.❞
—Rosalene Glickman

If you want to feel good...
Embrace change with a positive attitude

DISCOVER**MORE**

Dale Carnegie has a story about two men who were out chopping wood. One man worked hard all day, took no breaks and only stopped briefly for lunch. The other chopper took several breaks and a short nap at lunch. At the end of the day, the man who had taken no breaks was quite disturbed to see that the other had cut more wood than he had. He said, "I don't understand. Every time I looked around, you were sitting down, yet you cut more wood than I did."

His companion remarked, "Did you also notice that while sitting down, I was sharpening my axe?"

Proactively planning, rather than reacting to external conditions, makes moving through life smoother. It's an inside job. Sharpen your axe!

STAYING THE COURSE

Have you noticed that some of your friends welcome difficult challenges and others avoid them? What makes the difference? Resilience. It's a quality that develops over time by overcoming obstacles, solving problems and learning from mistakes.

>> Resilience helps you build stamina or staying power.

>> An important part of resilience is **flexibility**–your ability to adapt or respond to change.

>> It's your willingness to be flexible that can allow you to display **persistence**–which means staying the course, not giving up and having a willingness to strive.

>> **Resilience** is about your personal ability to turn setbacks into comebacks.

Because everyday life can produce all kinds of surprises, resilience is key to career success. Novices become experts by staying the course, learning from mistakes and making a personal commitment to use daily events as opportunities for personal improvement.

In the future, what if you're passed over for a promotion and a lesser-qualified applicant is selected instead? How do you come back from this setback? Follow the *Blueprint for Persisting Through Setbacks.*

"Attitude is a little thing that makes a big difference."
—Winston Churchill

BLUEPRINT FOR PERSISTING THROUGH SETBACKS

First	>> Face the problem
	>> Re-state the goal to be accomplished
Second	>> Choose alternative plans
	>> Re-assert control, commit to action
Third	>> Try again
	>> Re-focus action
Fourth	>> Stay the course
	>> Persist through adversity

In the creative world you're entering, you'll find opinions everywhere, many of them subjective. You'll want to build resilience in knowing that creative work has no hard and fast rules; what's beautiful to one person may not be to another. Or, pleasing one person might not be as easy as pleasing the next. Having resilience is the foundation for continually improving.

“ Anyone can give up; it's the easiest thing in the world to do. But to hold it together when everyone else would understand if you fell apart, that's true strength. **”**

—Unknown

LESSONS LEARNED

>> Integrity is the quality of being honest and having moral principles. It means doing what you say you will—not acting ethically only when it suits you.

>> Behaviors that destroy trust in work relationships include telling half-truths, seeking personal gain above shared gain, withholding important information, being closed to the ideas of others and acting inconsistently.

>> Making good life choices shapes the events of our lives, shows our character and creates our future.

>> Resilience is crucial for career success because it provides the stamina to stay the course by turning setbacks into comebacks.

»» 101ᶜ GLOSSARY/INDEX

Integrity 58
Being honest and having moral principles.

Mutual Respect 49
The respect two people feel for each other that feeds each person's need to feel valued.

Nutrition 6
The intake of appropriate dietary requirements.

Oral Hygiene 7
The act of maintaining healthy teeth and keeping the breath fresh.

Pelvic Tilt 16
A motion that keeps one from arching backward by bending the knees slightly and pulling in the abdominal muscles when reaching up.

Personal Ethics 51
A person's system of moral principles and values that develops from learning what is right or wrong.

Personal Hygiene 7
The individual system for maintaining cleanliness and health.

Personality 44
The outward reflection of inner thoughts, feelings, attitude and values.

Podiatrist 10
A foot doctor.

Posture 11, 27
The position of the body while standing, sitting and moving.

Professional Development 4
A commitment to constantly improving oneself.

Professional Ethics 51
The proper conduct one displays in relationships with employer, co-workers and clients.

Protein 6
Energy nutrient found in food and used by the body to make tissues such as muscle and hair.

Proximity 27
Nearness of another to one's personal space.

Public Hygiene 6
The codes of safety that protect the well-being of the public; example code areas include ventilation, lighting, disinfection and improper storage or use of food.

Resilience 57
The ability of a substance or object to spring back; the capacity to recover quickly from difficulties; toughness.

Respect 46
A feeling of deep admiration for someone or something.

Self-Esteem 46
Confidence and satisfaction in oneself.

Self-Respect 46
Pride in yourself and the assurance that you are behaving with honor and dignity.

Tact 30
The act of saying the proper thing to a person without giving offense.

Tendonitis 18
A condition that occurs when tendons get inflamed.

Trust 60
Ability to create relationships built upon mutual respect and openness.

Two-Way Communication 30
The act of listening and asking questions to gather information.

Verbal Communication 28
Refers to how one speaks by emphasizing the meaning of what one says through the tone or inflection of voice, level and rate of speech.

PIVOT POINT

 ACKNOWLEDGMENTS

Pivot Point Fundamentals is designed to provide education to undergraduate students to help prepare them for licensure and an entry-level position in the cosmetology field. An undertaking of this magnitude requires the expertise and cooperation of many people who are experts in their field. Pivot Point takes pride in our internal team of educators who develop cosmetology, esthetics and nails education, along with our print and digital experts, designers, editors, illustrators and video producers. Pivot Point would like to express our many thanks to these talented individuals who have devoted themselves to the business of beauty, lifelong learning and especially for help raising the bar for future professionals in our industry.

EDUCATION DEVELOPMENT | **Janet Fisher // Sabine Held-Perez // Vasiliki A. Stavrakis**
Markel Artwell
Eileen Dubelbeis
Brian Fallon
Melissa Holmes
Lisa Luppino
Paul Suttles
Amy Gallagher
Lisa Kersting
Jamie Nabielec
Vic Piccolotto
Ericka Thelin
Jane Wegner

EDITORIAL | **Maureen Spurr // Wm. Bullion // Deidre Glover**
Liz Bagby
Jack Bernin
Lori Chapman

DESIGN & PRODUCTION | **Jennifer Eckstein // Rick Russell // Danya Shaikh**
Joanna Jakubowicz
Denise Podlin
Annette Baase
Agnieszka Hansen
Kristine Palmer
Tiffany Wu

PROJECT MANAGEMENT | **Jenny Allen // Ken Wegrzyn**

DIGITAL DEVELOPMENT | John Bernin
Javed Fouch
Anna Fehr
Matt McCarthy
Marcia Noriega
Corey Passage
Herb Potzus

Pivot Point also wishes to take this opportunity to acknowledge the many contributors and product concept testers who helped make this program possible.

INDUSTRY CONTRIBUTORS

Linda Burmeister
Esthetics

Jeanne Braa Foster
Dr. Dean Foster
Eyes on Cancer

Mandy Gross
Nails

Andrea D. Kelly, MA, MSW
University of Delaware

Rosanne Kinley
Infection Control
National Interstate Council

Lynn Maestro
Cirépil by Perron Rigot, Paris

Andrzej Matracki
World and European
Men's Champion

MODERN SALON

Rachel Molepske
Look Good Feel Better, PBA
CUT IT OUT, PBA

Peggy Moon
Liaison to Regulatory and Testing

Robert Richards
Fashion Illustrations

Clif St. Germain, Ph.D
Educational Consultant

Andis Company

International Dermal Institute

HairUWear Inc.

Lock & Loaded Men's Grooming

PRODUCT CONCEPT TESTING

Central Carolina
Community College
Millington, North Carolina

Gateway Community Colleges
Phoenix, Arizona

MC College
Edmonton, Alberta

Metro Beauty Academy
Allentown, Pennsylvania

Rowan Cabarrus
Community College
Kannapolis, North Carolina

Sunstate Academy of
Cosmetology and Massage
Ft. Myers, Florida

Summit Salon Academy
Kokomo, Indiana

TONI&GUY Hairdressing Academy
Costa Mesa, California
Plano, Texas

Xenon Academy
Omaha, NE
Grand Island, NE

LEADERSHIP TEAM

Robert Passage
Chairman and CEO

Robert J. Sieh
Senior Vice President,
Finance and Operations

Judy Rambert
Vice President, Education

Kevin Cameron
Senior Vice President,
Education and Marketing

R.W. Miller
Vice President, Domestic Sales
and Field Education

Jan Laan
Vice President, International
Business Development

Katy O'Mahony
Director, Human Resources

In addition, we give special thanks to the North American Regulating agencies whose careful work protects us as well as our clients, enhancing the high quality of our work. These agencies include Occupational Health and Safety Agency (OSHA) and the U.S. Environmental Protection Agency (EPA). *Pivot Point Fundamentals*™ promotes use of their policies and procedures.

Pivot Point International would like to express our SPECIAL THANKS to the inspired visual artisans of Creative Commons, without whose talents this book of beauty would not be possible.

#MOOD